I0088053

First Family Trivia

Trivia On The Children Of The White House

Cheryl Pryor

Arlington & Amelia

Copyright © 2017 Cheryl Pryor

Arlington & Amelia Publishers

ArlingtonAmeliaPub@cfl.rr.com

All rights reserved. No portion of this book may be reproduced or transmitted by any form or by any means, electronic or mechanical, including photocopy, recording, or any information storage and retrieval system without permission from the author.

First Printing

ISBN:978-1-886541-16-0
ISBN:1-886541-16-7

For Perry

TABLE OF CONTENTS

Other Books By Cheryl Pryor

Children Of The Presidents

The Big Book of Presidential Trivia

The Big Book of First Ladies Trivia

The American Revolutionary War & The Birth of A Nation Trivia

Write Now

Legacy

The Wedding Survival Guide

Books For Children:

Trivia For Kids: The Presidents

Trivia For Kids: The First Ladies

The Sullivan Family Series

Savannah's Big Move

Savannah On Stage

Savannah On Horseback

Savannah In Look What Followed Me Home

Savannah And The Grumpy Neighbor

Savannah And The Mad Scientist

Savannah's World Travels Series

Savannah's Disney World Celebration

Savannah Goes To Paris

INTRODUCTION

This book follows my trivia books on the presidents and the first ladies, and now this book completes the series on the First Family with trivia on the children of the presidents.

Throughout this trivia book the children of the presidents, whether it is before or after the time their fathers were in the White House, will be referred to as the president's children, First Sons, or First Daughters.

The answers will be found at the end of each chapter. I found this to be the easiest way for you to test yourself without the answers being on the same page as the question – which sort of defeats the purpose of testing your knowledge.

If you find the children of the presidents a topic of interest, I would recommend my book *'Children of the Presidents,'* a book on the stories of the lives of the First Family members from childhood till their deaths and includes their time in the White House. If you're using this book as a trivia challenge, *'Children of the Presidents'* will definitely give you an advantage.

Before The Days In The White House

These events all occurred in the days before their father was the president

Answers for Chapter 1 are on page 6

1. Which president's daughter was baptized in China?

A. Dora Bush, daughter of George H W Bush
B. Chelsea Clinton, daughter of Bill Clinton
C. Sasha Obama, daughter of Barack Obama
D. Amy Carter, daughter of Jimmy Carter

2. Which presidential daughter was in a ballet recital where Michael Jackson came to see her perform?

A. Caroline Kennedy, daughter of John F. Kennedy
B. Jenna Bush, daughter of George W. Bush
C. Chelsea Clinton, daughter of Bill Clinton
D. Ivanka Trump, daughter of Donald Trump

3. She was the only daughter from her father's first marriage. Her mother died when she was two days old. Her father left her in the care of his sister and left for two years living out west driving cattle and hunting. Which future First Daughter was this?

A. Alice Roosevelt daughter of Theodore Roosevelt
B. Margaret Truman, daughter of Harry Truman
C. Maureen Reagan, daughter of Ronald Reagan
D. Nell Arthur, daughter of Chester Arthur

4. Which president's young daughter was cared for by a prisoner working on a trustee program who had received a life sentence for killing a man?

A. Chelsea Clinton, daughter of Bill Clinton
B. Patti Davis Reagan, daughter of Ronald Reagan
C. Amy Carter, daughter of Jimmy Carter
D. Dora Bush, daughter of George H W Bush

5. Which president's daughter, in the days before his presidency, was good friends with the stepdaughter of the Emperor Napoleon Bonaparte?

A. Lynda Johnson, daughter of Lyndon B Johnson
B. Eliza Monroe, daughter of James Monroe
C. Nellie Grant, daughter of Ulysses S. Grant
D. Ivanka Trump, daughter of Donald Trump

6. What is the name of the home where the stepchildren of George Washington lived?

A. Trump Tower
B. Monticello
C. Mount Vernon
D. Montpelier

7. Which presidential daughters stuffed paper down the toilets of the vice president's plane, Air Force Two, clogging them?

A. Barbara & Jenna Bush, daughters of George W Bush
B. Lynda & Luci Johnson, daughters of Lyndon B. Johnson
C. Ivanka & Tiffany Trump, daughters of Donald Trump
D. Julie & Tricia Nixon, daughters of Richard Nixon

8. Which presidential sons worked at their father's peanut farm in the years before his presidency?

A. George W & Jeb Bush, sons of George H W Bush
B. Michael & Ron Reagan, sons of Ronald Reagan
C. Jack & Chip Carter, sons of Jimmy Carter
D. Michael & Steve Ford, sons of Gerald Ford

9. Which presidential sons had their mouths washed out with soap by their mother when using foul language as young boys?

A. Sons of Donald Trump
B. Sons of George H W Bush
C. Sons of Jimmy Carter
D. Sons of Franklin D Roosevelt

10. At the age of thirteen, which presidential daughter decided to become a vegetarian?

A. Ivanka Trump, daughter of Donald Trump
B. Malia Obama, daughter of Barack Obama
C. Jenna Bush, daughter of George W Bush
D. Chelsea Clinton, daughter of Bill Clinton

11. Which presidential son was water boy for Stanford University's football team?

A. Herbert Hoover Jr, son of Herbert Hoover
B. Michael Reagan, son of Ronald Reagan
C. George W Bush, son of George H W Bush
D. Steve Ford, son of Gerald Ford

12. Which president while running for office had a picture of his dead daughter on his campaign buttons?

A. George H W Bush
B. John F Kennedy
C. William McKinley
D. Rutherford B Hayes

13. Which president's sons were taught sign language by their mother?

A. John & Cal Coolidge Jr, sons of Calvin Coolidge
B. Willie & Tad Lincoln, sons of Abraham Lincoln
C. Herbert Jr & Allan Hoover, sons of Herbert Hoover
D. Jack & Chip Carter, sons of Jimmy Carter

14. Which presidential child was head cheerleader while a senior in high school?

A. George W Bush, son of George H W Bush
B. Steve Ford, son of Gerald Ford
C. Barbara Bush, daughter of George W Bush
D. Jenna Bush, daughter of George W Bush

15. Two of which president's sons sailed with their father to Europe so he could help negotiate an end to the Revolutionary War?

A. Sons of Thomas Jefferson
B. Sons of John Adams
C. Sons of James Monroe
D. Sons of Franklin Pierce

16. While her father was vice president, which future president's daughter was threatened to be kidnapped by the SLA, Symbionese Liberation Army, the same group that kidnapped Patty Hearst the granddaughter of William Randolph Hearst?

A. Susan Ford, daughter of Gerald Ford
B. Chelsea Clinton, daughter of Bill Clinton
C. Patsy Washington, stepdaughter of George Washington
D. Maureen Reagan, daughter of Ronald Reagan

17. Which president's child was almost expelled from school for poor grades, using marijuana, and hashish?

A. Jeb Bush, son of George H W Bush
B. Malia Obama, daughter of Barack Obama
C. Ron Reagan, son of Ronald Reagan
D. Amy Carter, daughter of Jimmy Carter

18. By the age of two, which president's son had already traveled around the world twice?

A. George W Bush, son of George H W Bush
B. John F Kennedy Jr, son of John F. Kennedy
C. Herbert Hoover Jr, son of Herbert Hoover
D. John Eisenhower, son of Dwight D Eisenhower

19. Which president's son lost his father's inaugural address speech notes on their trip to Washington for the inauguration?

A. George W Bush, son of George H W Bush
B. Calvin Coolidge Jr, son of Calvin Coolidge
C. Robert Lincoln, son of Abraham Lincoln
D. Jacky Washington, son of George Washington

20. When his father was in Congress, this future presidential son remembered his father taking him to visit the U.S. Patent Office where they would spend hours in the Model Room looking at models of American inventions. His father would one day have a patented invention of his own. Who was the son of the only president to have a patent registered in his name?

A. Peter Jefferson, son of Thomas Jefferson
B. Andrew Jackson Jr, son of Andrew Jackson
C. Jeb Bush, son of George H W Bush
D. Robert Lincoln, son of Abraham Lincoln

Answers to Chapter 1

1. A - Doro Bush, daughter of George H W Bush

*While China banned freedom of worship to their own countrymen at this time (1975), Doro became the first person to ever be publicly baptized in the People's Republic of China since the days the Communist party took over the country in 1949.

2. D - Ivanka Trump, daughter of Donald Trump

*Michael Jackson was a neighbor living in Trump Towers at the time.

3. A – Alice Roosevelt, daughter of Theodore Roosevelt

4. C - Amy Carter, daughter of Jimmy Carter

5. B - Eliza Monroe, daughter of James Monroe

6. C - Mount Vernon

7. A - Barbara & Jenna Bush, daughters of George W Bush

8. C - Jack & Chip Carter, sons of Jimmy Carter

9. B – Sons of George H W Bush

10. D - Chelsea Clinton, daughter of Bill Clinton

11. A - Herbert Hoover Jr, son of Herbert Hoover

12. C - William McKinley

13. A - John & Cal Jr Coolidge, sons of Calvin Coolidge

14. A - George W Bush, son of George H W Bush

15. B – Sons of John Adams

16. A - Susan Ford, daughter of Gerald Ford

17. A - Jeb Bush, son of George H W Bush

18. C - Herbert Hoover Jr, son of Herbert Hoover

19. C - Robert Lincoln, son of Abraham Lincoln

* The notes were later found before the inauguration.

20. D – Robert Lincoln, son of Abraham Lincoln

2

Inauguration & Inaugural Events

Answers for Chapter 2 are on page 12

1. Which president's sons had to work the day their father was sworn into office for his first administration?

A. Abe Lincoln's sons
B. Calvin Coolidge's sons
C. Herbert Hoover's sons
D. None of the above

2. Which president's daughters were surprised to find the Jonas Brothers, a singing group, at the end of the scavenger hunt set up for them at the White House for them to enjoy while their parents attended inaugural balls?

A. Lyndon B. Johnson's daughters
B. Richard Nixon's daughters
C. George W. Bush's daughters
D. Barack Obama's daughters

3. Which president was the first to have his children attend his inauguration?

A. Martin Van Buren
B. John Tyler
C. John F. Kennedy
D. Lyndon B. Johnson

9

4. Which president didn't invite his son to his inauguration and in turn the son didn't attend his father's funeral?

A. Ron Reagan, son of Ronald Reagan
B. John Kennedy Jr, son of John F. Kennedy
C. Dick Taylor, son of Zachary Taylor
D. John Eisenhower, son of Dwight D Eisenhower

5. Which president along with his family was the first to get out of the presidential limo and walk to the White House during the inaugural parade?

A. John F Kennedy
B. James Monroe
C. Jimmy Carter
D. Warren Harding

6. Which First Daughter gave her father a thumbs-up sign after he took the oath of office?

A. Ivanka Trump
B. Sasha Obama
C. Chelsea Clinton
D. Susan Ford

7. Which president's son while working at Yellowstone as a park ranger was riding horseback patrol and oblivious to what was going on in the outside world was 'confiscated' by Secret Service agents, whisked aboard a helicopter, and rushed to the White House to attend his father's inauguration?

A. Michael Reagan
B. Archie Roosevelt
C. Alan Arthur
D. Jack Ford

8. Which First Son had to hold up his father and help him to the

rostrum to be sworn into office due to the fact that his father was handicapped?

A. Jeff Carter
B. Russell Harrison
C. Jimmy Roosevelt
D. Fred Grant

9. Which president's daughter was preparing for a date when her father telephoned changing her plans, where instead of going on a date she went to the Cabinet Room of the White House to witness her father sworn into office due to the death of the previous president?

A. Lynda Johnson
B. Martha Johnson
C. Nell Arthur
D. Margaret Truman

10. Name one of the president's sons (there were two) who was a college student at the time of his father's inauguration who had to turn around and return to college the morning after his father's inauguration, as his father didn't want him to miss school.

A. Allan Hoover
B. Jeb Bush
C. John Coolidge
D. John Eisenhower

Chapter 2 Answers

1. B - Calvin Coolidge's sons

*Vice President Calvin Coolidge was visiting at the home of his father when he was woken in the middle of the night to be informed the president was dead. Coolidge was sworn in immediately by his own father who was a notary public.

2. D - Malia & Sasha Obama

3. A - Martin Van Buren

4. C - Zachary Taylor

5. C - Jimmy Carter

6. B – Sasha Obama

7. D – Jack Ford

8. C – Jimmy Roosevelt

9. D – Margaret Truman

10. Either A or C would be correct

A - Allan Hoover

C – John Coolidge

3

Life In The White House

Answers for Chapter 3 are on page 20

1. Which president's son brought hungry children, which the White House kitchen called "street urchins," in to be fed at the White House?

A. Jacky Washington, son of George Washington
B. Elliott Roosevelt, son of Franklin D Roosevelt
C. Allan Hoover, son of Herbert Hoover
D. Tad Lincoln, son of Abraham Lincoln

2. Which president's son on his first night in the White House went on the roof with his stereo playing Led Zeppelin?

A. Chip Carter, son of Jimmy Carter
B. Donald Trump Jr, son of Donald Trump
C. Steve Ford, son of Gerald Ford
D. Michael Reagan, son of Ronald Reagan

3. Which president's daughter after staying overnight in the Lincoln Bedroom swore she had seen Lincoln's ghost?

A. Martha Jefferson, daughter of Thomas Jefferson
B. Mollie Garfield, daughter of James Garfield
C. Maureen Reagan, daughter of Ronald Reagan
D. Sasha Obama, daughter of Barack Obama

4. Which president's son had a butler replaced just because he didn't like the way he walked?

A. Allan Hoover, son of Herbert Hoover
B. Smith Van Buren, son of Martin Van Buren
C. Payne Madison, stepson of James Madison
D. Ron Reagan, son of Ronald Reagan

5. The first lady gave her daughters the advice, "Don't do anything you wouldn't mind seeing on the front page of the newspaper?" Which president's daughters received this advice?

A. Julie & Tricia Nixon, daughters of Richard Nixon
B. Lynda & Luci Johnson, daughters of Lyndon B Johnson
C. Malia & Sasha Obama, daughters of Barack Obama
D. Jessie & Margaret Wilson, daughters of Woodrow Wilson

6. Which president's daughter was reclusive to the point that her sister referred to her as, "the Howard Hughes of the White House?"

A. Caroline Kennedy, daughter of John F Kennedy
B. Amy Carter, daughter of Jimmy Carter
C. Luci Johnson, daughter of Lyndon B Johnson
D. Tricia Nixon, daughter of Richard Nixon

7. Which president's daughter had a pony named Macaroni that she rode on the White House lawn?

A. Ethel Roosevelt, daughter of Theodore Roosevelt
B. Eleanor Wilson, daughter of Woodrow Wilson
C. Anna Roosevelt, daughter of Franklin D Roosevelt
D. Caroline Kennedy, daughter of John F Kennedy

8. Two president's daughters were mocked on *Saturday Night Live.* Name one of them.

A. Chelsea Clinton, daughter of Bill Clinton
B. Jenna Bush, daughter of George W Bush
C. Patti Davis Reagan, daughter of Ronald Reagan
D. Amy Carter, daughter of Jimmy Carter

9. Which president's daughter was nicknamed 'Watusi Luci' by the press?

A. Tiffany Trump, daughter of Donald Trump
B. Luci Johnson, daughter of Lyndon B Johnson
C. Susan Ford, daughter of Gerald Ford
D. Jessie Wilson, daughter of Woodrow Wilson

10. Which presidential son's most memorable experience while living in the White House was to see a Wright Brother's flying machine land on the South Lawn of the White House?

A. Charlie Taft, son of William H Taft
B. Smith Van Buren, son of Martin Van Buren
C. Manning Force Hayes, son of Rutherford B Hayes
D. Archie Roosevelt, son of Theodore Roosevelt

11. Which president's daughter dated movie star George Hamilton?

A. Tricia Nixon, daughter of Richard Nixon
B. Margaret Truman, daughter of Harry Truman
C. Alice Roosevelt, daughter of Theodore Roosevelt
D. Lynda Johnson, daughter of Lyndon B Johnson

12. Which president's son carved his initials in the presidential yacht?

A. Chip Carter, son of Jimmy Carter
B. Tad Lincoln, son of Abraham Lincoln
C. Charlie Taft, son of William H Taft
D. None of the above

13. Which president's daughter was only the second in history to be an only child of a president?

A. Margaret Truman, daughter of Harry Truman
B. Luci Johnson, daughter of Lyndon B Johnson
C. Chelsea Clinton, daughter of Bill Clinton
D. Ivanka Trump, daughter of Donald Trump

14. Which president's sons were part of a group of friends called 'the White House Gang'?

A. Archie & Quintin Roosevelt, sons of Theodore Roosevelt
B. Tad & Willie Lincoln, sons of Abraham Lincoln
C. Rutherford Jr & Scott Hayes, sons of Rutherford B Hayes
D. All of the above

15. Which president's son tied goats to a chair and had them pull him through the East Room of the White House chariot style?

A. John Kennedy Jr, son of John F Kennedy
B. Quentin Roosevelt, son of Theodore Roosevelt
C. Tad Lincoln, son of Abraham Lincoln
D. Barron Trump, son of Donald Trump

16. Which president's sons and friends threw spitballs at President Andrew Jackson's portrait?

A. Sons of Theodore Roosevelt
B. Sons of Donald Trump
C. Sons of Franklin D Roosevelt
D. Sons of James Madison

17. Name the only two presidents to have a child born during their administration.

A. Thomas Jefferson & Grover Cleveland
B. Warren Harding & Bill Clinton
C. Grover Cleveland & John F Kennedy
D. None of the above

18. Which First Family member, along with the first lady, was taught to dance the Charleston by the White House butler – even though the president refused to let his family dance in public?

A. John Coolidge, son of Calvin Coolidge
B. Jessie Wilson, daughter of Woodrow Wilson
C. Caroline Kennedy, daughter of John F Kennedy
D. Herbert Hoover Jr, son of Herbert Hoover

19. During her father's administration, which president's daughter led marches for women's rights and organized protests and pushed her father into supporting the 19th Amendment giving women the right to vote?

A. Anna Roosevelt, daughter of Franklin D Roosevelt
B. Nell Arthur, daughter of Chester Arthur
C. Jessie Wilson, daughter of Woodrow Wilson
D. Alice Roosevelt, daughter of Theodore Roosevelt

20. Name one of the presidents sons who enjoyed going to the White House roof to watch the stars through a telescope.

A. Allan Hoover, son of Herbert Hoover
B. Marvin Bush, son of George H W Bush
C. Jeff Carter, son of Jimmy Carter
D. Jessie Grant, son of Ulysses S Grant

21. The young sons of a president were said to "run wild" in the White House. Which sons were they?

A. Abe Lincoln's sons
B. Theodore Roosevelt's sons

C. James Garfield's sons
D. All of the above

22. Which presidential daughter was scandalous, doing things such as smoking in public that young women of the times didn't do; yet the public and the press loved her wondering what scandalous thing she would do next?

A. Knoxie Taylor, daughter of Zachary Taylor
B. Nellie Grant, daughter of Ulysses S Grant
C. Alice Roosevelt, daughter of Theodore Roosevelt
D. Margaret Truman, daughter of Harry Truman

23. Which president's daughter gave a televised tour of the White House taking the viewers through private parts of the White House rarely seen by others on 'Sixty Minutes' with Harry Reasoner?

A. Tricia Nixon, daughter of Richard Nixon
B. Caroline Kennedy, daughter of John F Kennedy
C. Ivanka Trump, daughter of Donald Trump
D. Malia Obama, daughter of Barack Obama

24. Which president's daughter was taught to drive by the president at Camp David in an armored Secret Service car?

A. Chelsea Clinton, daughter of Bill Clinton
B. Malia Obama, daughter of Barack Obama
C. Tricia Nixon, daughter of Richard Nixon
D. Susan Ford, daughter of Gerald Ford

25. Which president's daughter milked the cows from the White House dairy every morning?

A. Nell Arthur, daughter of Chester Arthur
B. Martha Johnson, daughter of Andrew Johnson
C. Ruth Cleveland, daughter of Grover Cleveland

D. Elizabeth Monroe, daughter of James Monroe

Chapter 3 Answers

1. D – Tad Lincoln

2. C – Steve Ford

3. C – Maureen Reagan

4. A – Allan Hoover

5. B – Lynda & Luci Johnson

6. D – Tricia Nixon

7. D – Caroline Kennedy

8. Either answer is correct:
   A – Chelsea Clinton
   D – Amy Carter

9. B – Luci Johnson

10. A – Charlie Taft

11. D – Lynda Johnson

12. C – Charlie Taft

13. C – Chelsea Clinton

14. A – Archie & Quentin Roosevelt

15. C – Tad Lincoln

16. A – Sons of Roosevelt

17. C – Grover Cleveland & John F Kennedy

18. A – John Coolidge

19. C – Jessie Wilson

20. Either one is correct:
 C – Jeff Carter
 D – Jessie Grant

21. D – All of the above

22. C – Alice Roosevelt

23. A – Tricia Nixon

24. A – Chelsea Clinton

25. B – Martha Johnson

Holidays At The White House

Answers for Chapter 4 are on page 26

1. Which president's family spent each Christmas in Hawaii?

A. Donald Trump family
B. George H W Bush family
C. Franklin Roosevelt's family
D. Barack Obama family

2. Which was the first president to decorate the White House with a Christmas tree for his grandchildren?

A. Thomas Jefferson
B. Andrew Jackson
C. Benjamin Harrison
D. Franklin Roosevelt

3. Who was the first president whose daughters enjoyed the first Christmas tree in the White House decorated with electric lights?

A. Woodrow Wilson
B. Grover Cleveland
C. Andrew Johnson
D. John Tyler

4. Which former president's son went to a Halloween party dressed as Michelangelo's *David* covered in talcum powder and dressed only in a fig leaf?

A. Donald Trump Jr, son of Donald Trump
B. George W Bush, son of George H W Bush
C. John Kennedy Jr, son of John F Kennedy
D. Steve Ford, son of Gerald Ford

5. On Memorial Day, which First Daughter would join the first lady to decorate the graves of Civil War soldiers at Arlington National Cemetery?

A. Eliza Monroe
B. Fanny Hayes
C. Anna Roosevelt
D. Julie Nixon

6. Which president threw a Christmas party for his children and grandchildren that included an indoor "snowball fight"?

A. Andrew Jackson
B. Abraham Lincoln
C. Benjamin Harrison
D. George H W Bush

7. Which First Daughter received a talking doll for Christmas that was one day left in the Oval Office and inadvertently recorded the president using foul language?

A. Sasha Obama
B. Amy Carter
C. Caroline Kennedy
D. Nellie Grant

8. Which president's son was responsible for saving the turkey given to the White House for the president's Thanksgiving dinner, initiating the practice of pardoning the turkey?

A. John Kennedy, Jr
B. Tad Lincoln

C. Cal Coolidge, Jr
D. Quentin Roosevelt

9. The first lady wanted her children to experience the same joys as other children, so when Halloween came around she dressed up along with her children so as to not be recognized and took her children to a nearby neighborhood of the White House to go trick-or-treating. Which presidential children were these?

A. Children of James Garfield
B. Children of Theodore Roosevelt
C. Children of Grover Cleveland
D. Children of John F Kennedy

10. A Christmas tradition of which presidential family, did their father read Charles Dickens 'A Christmas Carol' to his children and grandchildren?

A. Franklin D Roosevelt
B. John F Kennedy
C. Lyndon B Johnson
D. Donald Trump

Chapter 4 Answers

1. D – Obama family

2. C – Benjamin Harrison

3. B – Grover Cleveland

4. C – John F Kennedy Jr

5. B – Fanny Hayes

6. A – Andrew Jackson

*The snowballs were specially fashioned cotton balls.

7. C – Caroline Kennedy

8. B – Tad Lincoln

*The turkey was named Jack and roamed freely on the White House grounds.

9. D – Children of John F Kennedy
* They might have been able to pull it off if it weren't for all the Secret Service agents with them.

10. A - Franklin D Roosevelt

Traveling With The First Family

Answers for Chapter 5 are on page 30

1. Which presidential daughter was presented to King George III, the king responsible for the colonies fighting for their independence?

A. Eliza Madison
B. Louisa Catherine Adams
C. Maria Jefferson
D. Nabby Adams

2. Which president's children, during their White House days, traveled abroad more than any other presidential children?

A. Herbert Hoover's children
B. Donald Trump's children
C. John F Kennedy's children
D. Barack Obama's children

3. Which president and son explored the Amazon?

A. Theodore Roosevelt and son Kermit
B. Zachary Taylor and son Dick
C. Franklin Pierce and son Benjamin
D. Herbert Hoover and son Herbert Jr

4. What future president's son was thought to be lost at sea for five months and presumed dead?

A. Charles Adams
B. Barron Trump
C. Allan Hoover
D. Chester Alan Chester Jr

5. Who was the first president, who along with the first lady and two sons, was the first sitting president to travel to the West Coast?

A. Herbert Hoover
B. Rutherford B Hayes
C. Theodore Roosevelt
D. William Henry Harrison

6. Which 2 presidential sons while on an expedition to Asia confirmed the existence of the giant panda – the first men from the west to do so?

A. Ted Jr and Kermit Roosevelt
B. Don Jr and Eric Trump
C. Abraham and John Van Buren
D. Richard and Francis Cleveland

7. In 1905, the president sent his daughter along on a diplomatic delegation as a goodwill ambassador, the *first* First Daughter to ever serve in this role, on a four month voyage to Asia. Who was she?

A. Caroline Kennedy
B. Martha Jefferson
C. Maureen Reagan
D. Alice Roosevelt

8. While traveling with the president and first lady to Africa to launch the President's emergency Plan for AIDS relief, which First Daughter later described the trip as life-changing? She became founder and CEO of Global Health Corps as a result.

A. Barbara Bush
B. Chelsea Clinton
C. Tricia Nixon
D. Caroline Kennedy

9. Which First Daughter traveled with her father, the sitting president, for a secret meeting with Churchill and Stalin at Yalta?

A. Daughter of Harry Truman, Margaret
B. Daughter of Franklin D Roosevelt, Anna
C. Daughter of Lyndon B Johnson, Luci
D. Daughter of Donald Trump, Ivanka

10. Which president's son while part of a group sponsored by the National outdoor Leadership Course in Africa had to evade a charging rhinocerous and got lost in the snake-infested African bush and a search party of Masai warriors were sent out to search for them. Who was this son of a president?

A. Steve Ford
B. Jeb Bush
C. Eric Trump
D. John F Kennedy, Jr

Chapter 5 Answers

1. D – Nabby Adams

2. Barack Obama's children

3. A – Theodore Roosevelt & son Kermit

4. A – Charles Adams

* His father was sending him from England back to America. Originally he had an escort, but the ship had to divert to Spain for repairs where his escort left him in a strange country where he didn't speak the language. Eventually he made it home, but by then his family had feared him dead and lost at sea.

5. B – Rutherford B Hayes

6. A- Ted Jr & Kermit Roosevelt

7. D – Alice Roosevelt

8. A – Barbara Bush

9. B – Daughter of Franklin D Roosevelt, Anna

10. D – John F Kennedy, Jr

6

The First Or The Only One To Do So

Answers for Chapter 6 are on page 35

1. Which First Daughter was the first Orthodox Jewish First Daughter?

A. Daughter of George Washington
B. Daughter of Donald Trump
C. Daughter of William H Harrison
D. Daughter of John Tyler

2. Which presidential sons were the first Boy Scouts to live in the White House?

A. Willie & Tad Lincoln
B. Harry & Abram Garfield
C. John & Cal Coolidge Jr
D. Allan & Herbert Hoover Jr

3. Who is the only president to have two of his children born during his administration?

A. Grover Cleveland
B. John F Kennedy
C. Franklin Pierce
D. None of the above

4. Which was the first presidential daughter to assume the role of hostess for the White House?

A. Martha Jefferson

B. Ivanka Trump
C. Martha Johnson
D. Eliza Monroe

5. Who was the first son of a president to have been in Little League? Hint: He would one day be part owner of a baseball team.

A. Eric Trump
B. George W Bush
C. Ron Reagan
D. Michael Ford

6. Who is the only presidential daughter to have had her prom in the White House?

A. Malia Obama
B. Chelsea Clinton
C. Amy Carter
D. Susan Ford

7. The first child born in the White House was the son of which presidential daughter?

A. Patsy Washington
B. Nabby Adams
C. Martha Jefferson
D. Nellie Grant

8. Which president's daughter was the first and only child of a president born in the White House?

A. Pearl Tyler
B. Fanny Hayes
C. Esther Cleveland
D. Margaret Truman

9. Which president's daughters were the first African-Americans

to live in the White House?

A. Daughters of Andrew Johnson
B. Daughters of William H Harrison
C. Daughters of Zachary Taylor
D. Daughters of Barack Obama

10. Which president's adult children and grandchildren were the first to eat ice cream?

A. George Washington
B. Andrew Jackson
C. Abe Lincoln
D. Thomas Jefferson

11. Which president's daughter was the first to have her wedding take place at the White House?

A. Maria Monroe
B. Alice Tyler
C. Nellie Grant
D. Alice Roosevelt

12. Who was the first presidential son to also become president?

A. George W Bush
B. Abraham Van Buren
C. John Quincy Adams
D. Benjamin Harrison

13. Which two president's sons became the first brothers to be simultaneous governors?

A. Herbert Jr & Allan Hoover
B. Quentin & Archie Roosevelt
C. George W & Jeb Bush
D. John & Smith Van Buren

14. Which president's son was the first child ever born to a President-elect?

A. Son of Thomas Jefferson
B. Son of James Madison
C. Son of James Buchanan
D. Son of John F Kennedy

15. Which president's stepson was the first member of a presidential family to end up in debtor's prison due to gambling debts?

A. Jacky Washington
B. Payne Madison
C. Charles Adams
D. Benjamin Pierce

Chapter 6 Answers

1. B – Daughter of Donald Trump

2. C – John & Cal Coolidge, Jr

3. A – Grover Cleveland

4. A – Martha Jefferson

5. B – George W Bush

6. D – Susan Ford

7. C – Martha Jefferson

8. C – Esther Cleveland

9. D – Daughters of Barack Obama

10. D - Thomas Jefferson

11. A – Maria Monroe

12. C – John Quincy Adams

13. C - George W & Jeb Bush

14. D – Son of John F Kennedy

15. B – Payne Madison

7

Do You Know...

Answers for Chapter 7 are on page 41

1. Which First Son's life was saved by the brother of the man who would later assassinate his father during his presidency?

A. Michael Reagan
B. Robert Lincoln
C. Quentin Cleveland
D. Harry Garfield

2. Which president had the most children? (He had 15 children.)

A. George H W Bush
B. Jimmy Carter
C. John Tyler
D. Zachary Taylor

3. The Baby Ruth candy bar was supposedly named after the daughter of a president. Who was she?

A. Daughter of Grover Cleveland
B. Daughter of Warren Harding
C. Daughter of Franklin D Roosevelt
D. Daughter of Harry Truman

4. Which presidential daughter and her immediate family, as of the year 2017, are worth $500 million?

A. Ivanka Trump
B. Chelsea Clinton

C. Caroline Kennedy
D. None of the above

5. Which president's son tracked grizzly bears while working for the National Geographic Society?

A. Dick Taylor
B. Kermit Roosevelt
C. Charles Taft
D. Steve Ford

6. Which president's daughter while working as an assistant teacher came to school dressed as Dr. Seuss' *The Cat In The Hat*'?

A. Julie Nixon
B. Doro Bush
C. Margaret Truman
D. Jenna Bush

7. Which two president's children's mother was the famous actress Jane Wyman?

A. Maureen & Michael Reagan
B. Susan & Jack Ford
C. Eleanor & Jessie Wilson
D. Don Jr & Eric Trump

8. Which president's son did the press nickname "John-John"?

A. Son of Jimmy Carter
B. Son of John F Kennedy
C. Son of Dwight D Eisenhower
D. Son of William H Taft

9. How many presidential children were an only child?

A. 1
B. 3
C. 2
D. 5

10. Which presidential son, while president himself, went skinny-dipping in the Potomac River?

A. George W Bush
B. Bill Clinton
C. Benjamin Harrison
D. John Quincy Adams

11. Which First Daughter was charged by a 6,000 lb pet runaway elephant at a pet show and was saved by a Secret Service agent?

A. Sasha Obama
B. Jenna Bush
C. Amy Carter
D. Tricia Nixon

12. Which First Daughter at the time she moved into the White House was the youngest child of a president since John F Kennedy's son?

A. Amy Carter
B. Chelsea Clinton
C. Barron Trump
D. Sasha Obama

13. Which First Son did not move into the White House immediately after his father became president so he could finish his school year without having to change schools?

A. Smith Van Buren
B. Cal Coolidge, Jr
C. John Eisenhower

D. Barron Trump

14. Which president's son after graduating from college moved out west and lived out of the back of his truck for about a year and a half?

A. Don Trump, Jr
B. Steve Ford
C. Jeb Bush
D. Allan Hoover

15. Who is currently the oldest living First Family member (as of the year 2017)?

A. Caroline Kennedy
B. Lynda Johnson
C. John Eisenhower
D. Ron Reagan

Chapter 7 Answers

1. B - Robert Lincoln

2. C - John Tyler

3. A - Daughter of Grover Cleveland

* From the book: 'Children of the Presidents' by Cheryl Pryor:
There is a story that has been told to which people still believe to be true today; and that is that the Baby Ruth candy bar was named after Ruth Cleveland. That may or may not be the case; it is what the Curtiss Candy Company insisted on when taken to court by Babe Ruth the baseball player for infringing on his name.

It was in the early 1920's when the candy bar came out, which was seventeen years after the death of Ruth Cleveland and over two decades after her father left office. Babe Ruth however was a famous baseball player who was having a tremendous year having hit fifty-four home runs. But, if the candy bar company admitted it was named after Babe Ruth they would have had to pay him for the use of his name.

4. C - Caroline Kennedy

5. D - Steve Ford

6. D - Jenna Bush

7. A - Maureen & Michael Reagan

8. B - Son of John F Kennedy

9. 2

* They were Margaret Truman and Chelsea Clinton

10. D - John Quincy Adams

11. C - Amy Carter

12. D – Sasha Obama

13. Barron Trump

14. Don Trump, Jr

15. B – Lynda Johnson

8

College Days

Answers for Chapter 8 are on page 46

1. Which First Daughter has the highest educational credentials to date?

A. Caroline Kennedy
B. Chelsea Clinton
C. Tiffany Trump
D. Lynda Johnson

2. Which First Daughter attended Yale becoming the 4th generation of her family and the first female from her family to attend the Ivy League university?

A. Ivanka Trump
B. Chelsea Clinton
C. Barbara Bush
D. Malia Obama

3. Which president's son was a member of the Skull and Bones secret club at Yale?

A. Dick Taylor
B. Robert Taft
C. George W Bush
D. All of the above

4. As this presidential son was receiving his diploma from West Point, his father the Supreme Allied Commander of WWII was

overseeing the invasion of the beaches of Normandy known as D-Day. Who was he?

A. Fred Grant
B. Jeb Bush
C. Robert Lincoln
D. John Eisenhower

5. Which president's son attended West Point military school?

A. Martin Van Buren
B. Fred Grant
C. John Eisenhower
D. All of the above

6. Which First Son having just moved into the White House changed his original plans to study oceanography at Duke University and instead moved out west to become a cowboy?

A. Steve Ford
B. Ron Reagan
C. Fred Grant
D. John Kennedy, Jr

7. A student at Yale, which First Son while attending the Yale/Princeton game was one of the spectators after the game who attempted to destroy the vintage wooden goalposts and was caught in the act by the police?

A. Robert Lincoln
B. George W Bush
C. Franklin Roosevelt, Jr
D. Cal Coolidge, Jr

8. Which First Son went to seminary school and became an ordained minister?

A. Ron Reagan

B. Neil Bush
C. Michael Ford
D. John Eisenhower

9. Which First Daughter arrived at Stanford University as a new college student with an entourage including the president, first lady, dozens of Secret Service agents, and over 200 reporters?

A. Chelsea Clinton
B. Amy Carter
C. Julie Nixon
D. Caroline Kennedy

10. Which First Son dropped out of Yale his first semester to become a ballet dancer?

A. Eric Trump
B. George W Bush
C. Ron Reagan
D. Jack Ford

Chapter 8 Answers

1. B – Chelsea Clinton

2. C – Barbara Bush

3. D – All of the above

4. D – John Eisenhower

5. D – All of the above

6. A – Steve Ford

7. B – George W Bush

8. C – Michael Ford

9. A – Chelsea Clinton

10. C – Ron Reagan

9

Grandchildren of the Presidents

Answers for Chapter 9 are on page 50

1. The grandson of which president built Arlington House which later became part of Arlington Cemetery?

A. George Washington
B. Thomas Jefferson
C. James Madison
D. Abraham Lincoln

2. Which pre-Civil War president who was born during George Washington's administration has two grandsons still living today (as of the year 2017)?

A. Zachary Taylor
B. Thomas Jefferson
C. Abraham Lincoln
D. John Tyler

3. Which president's grandson also became a president?

A. John Adams
B. William H Harrison
C. Andrew Johnson
D. Theodore Roosevelt

4. Which president's grandson had Camp David named after him? Hint: He married a president-elect's daughter.

A. Grover Cleveland

47

B. Franklin D Roosevelt
C. Dwight D Eisenhower
D. William McKinley

5. True or False. After Washington's stepson Jacky died, George and Martha raised Jacky's two youngest children.

6. During which president's administration did his grandson live at the White House and became "the most famous baby in the world," according to the press?

A. Millard Fillmore
B. Franklin Roosevelt
C. Ulysses S Grant
D. Benjamin Harrison

7. Which president had a grandchild that was deaf?

A. Cal Coolidge
B. James Monroe
C. Abraham Lincoln
D. Jimmy Carter

8. The granddaughter of which president married a prince in Russia making her a 'bona fide' princess?

A. Ulysses S Grant
B. James Garfield
C. Herbert Hoover
D. William H Taft

9. George and Martha Washington's two grandchildren who lived with them, Nelly and Wash, joined them when their grandfather became president to live in what city, which was the nation's first capital?

A. New York City

B. Philadelphia
C. Boston
D. Washinton, D.C.

10. The great-granddaughter of which president was married to Civil War General Robert E. Lee?

A George Washington
B. Zachary Taylor
C. Ulysses S Grant
D. Abraham Lincoln

Chapter 9 Answers

1. A - George Washington

2. D - John Tyler

3. B William H Harrison

4. C - Dwight D Eisenhower

5. True

6. D - Benjamin Harrison

* The baby was known as Baby McKee

7. B - James Monroe

8. A - Ulysses S Grant

*President Grant's granddaughter Julia, the daughter of his son Fred, became a Russian princess. The prince she married came from one of the oldest and richest in the Russian empire. She and her family had to flee Russia during the Russian Revolution with her jewels sewn into her clothing. They moved to the U.S. and settled in Florida. She wrote of her tales of fleeing from the Russian Revolution. The book is titled 'Revolutionary Days' by Princess Julia Cantacuzene.

9. B - Philadelphia

10. A - George Washington

10

Presidential Pets

Answers for Chapter 10 are on page 54

1. Which First Daughter had a cat named Misty Malarky Ying Yang?

A. Amy Carter
B. Chelsea Clinton
C. Caroline Kennedy
D. Susan Ford

2. Which First Family had a Golden Retriever named Liberty that had puppies while living in the White House?

A Reagan family
B. Garfield family
C. Ford family
D. Franklin D Roosevelt family

3. Which First Daughter had a cat named Socks?

A Tricia Nixon
B. Sasha Obama
C. Chelsea Clinton
D. Jenna Bush

4. Which First Family had 2 Portuguese water dogs, one named Bo and the other named Sunny?

A Lyndon B Johnson family
B. Obama family

C. Coolidge family
D. Carter family

5. Which president's son kept 2 pet alligators at the White House?

A. Allan Hoover
B. Barron Trump
C. George W Bush
D. Elliott Roosevelt

6. Which president kept a goat named Old Whiskers who pulled his grandchildren around in a cart?

A. Abraham Lincoln
B. Benjamin Harrison
C. John Tyler
D. George Washington

7. Which First Daughter had a pet green garter snake named Emily Spinach she often wore draped around her neck?

A. Margaret Truman
B. Ivanka Trump
C. Alice Roosevelt
D. Malia Trump

8. Which First Son had a pet kangaroo rat that would hop across the table to the president to be fed a lump of sugar?

A. John F Kennedy, Jr
B. Kermit Roosevelt
C. Allan Hoover
D. Cal Coolidge, Jr

9. Abraham Lincoln promised his young sons ponies if he won the presidency, which presidential hopeful promised his

daughters a dog if he won; and he did?

A. Richard Nixon
B. Barack Obama
C. Lyndon B Johnson
D. George W Bush

10. Which First Son took his pony Algonquin up in the White House elevator and into the private quarters to cheer up his sick brother?

A. Fred Grant
B. Harry Garfield
C. Russell Harrison
D. Quentin Roosevelt

Chapter 10 Answers

1. A - Amy Carter

2. C – Ford family

3. C – Chelsea Clinton

4. B – Obama family

5. A – Allan Hoover

6. B - Benjamin Harrison

* One day the goat while pulling the president's grandson in the cart on the grounds of the White House escaped with the president running down Pennsylvania Avenue chasing the goat and his grandson.

7. C – Alice Roosevelt

8. B – Kermit Roosevelt

9. B – Barack Obama

10. D – Quentin Roosevelt

11

Romance & Weddings

Answers for Chapter 11 are on page 58

1. Who was the *first* First Daughter to be married at the White House?

A. Maria Jefferson
B. Maria Monroe
C. Alice Tyler
D. Martha Johnson

2. Which president-elect's daughter married the grandson of a former president?

A. Caroline Kennedy
B. Margaret Truman
C. Knoxie Taylor
D. Julie Nixon

3. Which sitting president's daughter once dated a future president, but they did not hit it off?

A. Luci Johnson
B. Tricia Nixon
C. Mollie Garfield
D. Nellie Grant

4. Which First Son married the first girl he ever dated, a girl from Mexico who spoke no English?

A. Eric Trump

B. Elliott Roosevelt
C. Dick Taylor
D. Jeb Bush

5. Which president is the only one to have 2 daughters get married at the White House?

A. Lyndon B Johnson
B. Woodrow Wilson
C. George W Bush
D. Richard Nixon

6. Which First Daughter is the only one to have her wedding take place at Camp David?

A. Lynda Johnson
B. Caroline Kennedy
C. Doro Bush
D. Chelsea Clinton

7. Who is the only First Daughter to have her wedding take place in the Rose Garden at the White House?

A. Alice Roosevelt
B. Nellie Grant
C. Lynda Johnson
D. Tricia Nixon

8. Who was the *first* First Daughter to be married in a church while her father was president?

A. Maria Monroe
B. Nellie Grant
C. Margaret Truman
D. Luci Johnson

9. Which First Daughter was the first to cut her wedding cake

with the sword of a White House aide?

A. Alice Roosevelt
B. Luci Johnson
C. Caroline Kennedy
D. Mollie Garfield

10. Which president's daughter married Jefferson Davis who would one day be president of the Confederate States?

A. Knoxie Taylor
B. Mollie Garfield
C. Pearl Tyler
D. Abbie Fillmore

11. Which president is the only president to have a son who married in the White House?

A. John Quincy Adams
B. James Buchanan
C. Franklin Pierce
D. Woodrow Wilson

12. Who was the *last* First Daughter to be married at the White House?

A. Anna Roosevelt
B. Margaret Truman
C. Lynda Johnson
D. Jenna Bush

1. B – Maria Monroe

2. D – Julie Nixon

3. B- Tricia Nixon

* Tricia Nixon once went on a date with George W Bush when he was in the National Guard. The date had been set up by his father, also a future president who at the time was working in the Nixon administration. The date did not go well and immediately after dinner Tricia asked George to take her home.

4. D – Jeb Bush

5. B – Woodrow Wilson

* Lyndon B Johnson also had two daughters marry during his administration, but only one of his daughters had her wedding at the White House.

6. C – Doro Bush

7. D – Tricia Nixon

8. D – Luci Johnson

9. A – Alice Roosevelt

10. A – Knoxie Taylor

11. A – John Quincy Adams

12. C – Lynda Johnson

12

War

Answers for Chapter 12 are on page 62

1. Which First Son, a general, volunteered to lead the assault in the first wave of attacks at Normandy on D-Day?

A. John Eisenhower
B. John Coolidge
C. Ted Roosevelt, Jr
D. Richard Cleveland

2. Which First Son at the age of seven witnessed the Battle of Bunker Hill from a hilltop near his home?

A. Jacky Washington
B. Charles Johnson
C. Alan Arthur
D. John Quincy Adams

3. General Patton described which First Son as "one of the bravest men I've ever known"?

A. Ted Roosevelt, Jr
B. Webb Hayes
C. George W Bush
D. Ron Reagan

4. Which president's 2 daughters lived at the White House while their husbands were in Vietnam and had to listen to protestors

outside the White House?

A. George W Bush
B. Ronald Reagan
C. Richard Nixon
D. Lyndon B Johnson

5. Which First Daughter traveled to Europe during WWI singing and putting on concerts to entertain the troops?

A. Margaret Wilson
B. Alice Roosevelt
C. Mollie Garfield
D. Margaret Truman

6. Which president's son was shot down by a German fighter pilot?

A. John Kennedy, Jr
B. Quentin Roosevelt
C. Charles Taft
D. John Coolidge

7. Which presidential son helped negotiate the end of the War of 1812?

A. John Quincy Adams
B. Payne Madison
C. Peter Jefferson
D. Don Trump, Jr

8. Which president's son was General Omar Bradley referring to when he said his fighting and leadership during D-Day was "the single bravest act" he witnessed during the entire war?

A. Ron Reagan
B. Robert Lincoln
C. John Eisenhower

D. Ted Roosevelt, Jr

9. Which sitting president's son joined the army during the Civil War?

A. Robert Lincoln
B. Andrew Johnson, Jr
C. Fred Grant
D. John Tyler, Jr

10. Which president, in his pre-presidential days, took his eleven-year old son with him while fighting in the Civil War?

A. Zachary Taylor
B. Abraham Lincoln
C. Ulysses S Grant
D. William H Harrison

11. During what war did George Washington's stepson die after suffering from camp fever which is a form of dysentery soldiers in camp suffered with?

A. Revolutionary War
B. French & Indian War
C. Civil War
D. War of 1812

12. Which presidential son flew in Eddie Rickenbacker's squadron during WWI?

A. John Eisenhower
B. Quentin Roosevelt
C. Robert Taft
D. Herbert Hoover, Jr

Chapter 12 Answers

1. C - Ted Roosevelt, Jr

*From 'Children of the Presidents' by Cheryl Pryor: Ted served during WWII as a brigadier general. When he learned of the attack that was to take place on Utah Beach he put in a request to lead the assault. His request was denied more than once and was told there would be no generals taking part in the assault. Ted continued the fight to be a part of the invasion stating that to have a general land in the first wave of attacks at Normandy would boost morale for the men who would most certainly be on a suicide mission. Eventually it was agreed he could take part, but only after it was made very clear that his chances of survival were practically nonexistent.

It wasn't just the fact that he was a general or the son of a president, but he was 56 years old and suffering from battle wounds from the last world war and couldn't walk without the aid of a walking stick. But, he did indeed lead the assault standing on the beach with bullets flying around his head directing his troops to their positions. He was a courageous and inspirational leader for the troops he led that day; and yes, he did survive.

2. D - John Quincy Adams

3. A - Ted Roosevelt, Jr

4. D - Lyndon B Johnson

5. A - Margaret Wilson

6. B - Quentin Roosevelt

7. A - John Quincy Adams

8. D - Ted Roosevelt, Jr

9. A - Robert Lincoln

10. C - Ulysses S Grant

11. A - Revolutionary War

12. B – Quentin Roosevelt

13

Scandals Involving The First Family

Answers for Chapter 13 are on page 70

1. Which president's son was accused of being involved in an assassination plot?

A. Chip Carter
B. Herbert Hoover, Jr
C. Chester Arthur, Jr
D. Elliott Roosevelt

2. Which president's son had his mother committed to an insane asylum?

A. Payne Madison
B. George W Bush
C. Russell Harrison
D. Robert Lincoln

3. Which president's son was arrested for DUI?

A. Payne Madison
B. John Eisenhower
C. George W Bush
D. Barron Trump

4. Which First Daughter posed nude for Playboy magazine?

A. Ivanka Trump
B. Tricia Nixon
C. Susan Ford
D. Patti Davis Reagan

5. Which daughter of a sitting president was a college student when the Monica Lewinsky scandal involving the president made national news?

A. Luci Johnson
B. Patti Davis Reagan
C. Malia Obama
D. Chelsea Clinton

6. While the president and first lady had no children from their marriage, he had an illegitimate daughter with a woman he continued having an affair with even during his time in the White House. He supported the illegitimate daughter, but refused to ever see her. Who was the president?

A. Bill Clinton
B. John F Kennedy
C. Warren Harding
D. James Buchanan

7. Which president's five children had 19 marriages between them?

A. Jimmy Carter
B. Franklin D Roosevelt
C. George H W Bush
D. Gerald Ford

8. Which president's son was involved in the 1988 Silverado Savings & Loan scandal?

A. Michael Reagan
B. Neil Bush
C. Don Trump, Jr
D. Franklin Roosevelt, Jr

9. Which First Daughter was abused by her first husband?

A. Doro Bush
B. Maureen Reagan
C. Caroline Kennedy
D. Ethel Roosevelt

10. Which First Daughter's father was only the second president in history to be impeached?

A. Martha Johnson
B. Chelsea Clinton
C. Amy Carter
D. Caroline Kennedy

11. Which 2 First Daughters had to face the humiliation of their father being the only president in U.S. history to resign?

A. Lyndon B Johnson's daughters
B. George W Bush's daughters
C. Richard Nixon's daughters
D. Woodrow Wilson's daughters

12. Which First Daughter had a daughter not of her husbands, but fathered by a senator she was having an affair with?

A. Patti Davis Reagan
B. Ruth Cleveland
C. Fanny Hayes
D. Alice Roosevelt

13. Which First Daughter claimed her mother, the first lady, mentally and physically abused her?

A. Chelsea Clinton
B. Patti Davis Reagan
C. Amy Carter
D. Caroline Kennedy

14. Which First Sons smoked dope in the White House leaving bongs laying about?

A. Sons of George H W Bush
B. Sons of Jimmy Carter
C. Sons of Gerald Ford
D. Sons of Herbert Hoover

15. Which First Daughter is involved in her family's foundation that during her mother's 2nd run for the presidency it was "strongly" suggested that foreign governments 'paid to play'?

A. Ivanka Trump
B. Chelsea Clinton
C. Jenna Bush
D. Lynda Johnson

16. Which president had two children whose ex-spouses committed suicide and another attempted suicide?

A. John Quincy Adams
B. Franklin D Roosevelt
C. Zachary Taylor
D. James Garfield

17. Which First Son ran for the presidency twice unsuccessfully? In his last run for the presidency in 2016 he pledged on national television that he would endorse the Republican candidate left standing at the end, but he did not do so showing the country he was not a man of his word. Who is he?

A. Jeb Bush
B. John Kennedy, Jr
C. Elliott Roosevelt
D. George W Bush

18. Which First Son was sexually abused as a young child by a camp counselor?

A. Jimmy Roosevelt
B. Jeff Carter
C. George W Bush
D. Michael Reagan

19. Which First Son received a "less than honorable" discharge from the navy after being involved in a drug bust?

A. Eric Trump
B. George W Bush
C. Jack Carter
D. John Eisenhower

20. Which 2 First Daughters caught the media's attention with using a fake ID and being caught in underage drinking?

A. Ivanka & Tiffany Trump
B. Malia & Sasha Obama
C. Barbara & Jenna Bush
D. Maureen & Patti Reagan

Chapter 13 Answers

1. D - Elliott Roosevelt

*From the book 'Children of the Presidents' by Cheryl Pryor: Elliott Roosevelt was accused of being involved in an assassination plot on the Bahamanian Prime Minister. He offered $100,000 to an alleged mobster front man to assassinate the prime minister paying him $10,000 up front. The check with his signature was produced along with taped conversations. Elliott maintained up until his death that it wasn't true. He was investigated by the Senate in 1973 of his ties to organized crime.

2. D - Robert Lincoln

3. C - George W Bush

4. D - Patti Davis Reagan

5. D - Chelsea Clinton

6. C - Warren Harding

7. B - Franklin D Roosevelt

8. B - Neil Bush

9. B - Maureen Reagan

10. B - Chelsea Clinton

11. C - Richard Nixon's daughters

12. D - Alice Roosevelt

13. B - Patti Davis Reagan

14. B - Jimmy Carter

15. B - Chelsea Clinton

16. B – Franklin D Roosevelt

17. A – Jeb Bush

18. D – Michael Reagan

19. C – Jack Carter

20. C – Barbara & Jenna Bush

History In The Making

Answers for Chapter 14 are on page 77

1. Which president's son was there to witness the signing of the Treaty of Paris which officially ended the Revolutionary War and recognized America's independence?

A. Jacky Washington
B. John Quincy Adams
C. Peter Jefferson
D. Payne Madison

2. During their grandfather's presidency is when the Lewis and Clark expedition took place, so which president's grandchildren were able to view specimens and items collected during the expedition?

A. Thomas Jefferson
B. James Madison
C. James Monroe
D. Rutherford B Hayes

3. The son of which president was sent to England as a representative of the U.S. for the coronation of Queen Victoria?

A. James Madison
B. Martin Van Buren
C. James Polk
D. Millard Fillmore

4. Which First Daughter was one of only five American women

permitted to witness the historic signing of the Versailles Treaty?

A. Martha Jefferson
B. Eliza Monroe
C. Anna Roosevelt
D. Margaret Wilson

5. Which presidential children were living in the White House when the first telephone was installed?

A. Abby & Powers Fillmore
B. Alan & Nell Arthur
C. Scott & Fanny Hayes
D. Tad & Willie Lincoln

6. Which president's son was in China during the Boxer Rebellion as part of the relief force that rescued trapped Westerners in Peking, including a future president and first lady?

A. Robert Lincoln
B. Fred Grant
C. John Eisenhower
D. Webb Hayes

7. Which First Daughters' father was president at the time 9-11 took place?

A. Barbara & Jenna Bush
B. Malia & Sasha Obama
C. Julie & Tricia Nixon
D. Lynda & Luci Johnson

8. Which First Daughter's father ordered the use of atomic bombs on Hiroshima and Nagasaki?

A. Anna Roosevelt
B. Margaret Truman
C. Caroline Kennedy

D. Jessie Wilson

9. Which presidential family's father was the first to become vice president under the 25th amendment and became the first to become president without a single popular or electoral vote?

A. The family of Lyndon B Johnson
B. The family of Harry Truman
C. The family of Gerald Ford
D. The family of Chester Arthur

10. Which president's daughter was married to the attorney who served as prosecutor in the trial of Aaron Burr for treason?

A. Patsy Washington
B. Letty Tyler
C. Maria Jefferson
D. Eliza Monroe

11. What young presidential son traveled with the troops during the Civil War witnessing battles and life as a soldier?

A. Dick Taylor
B. Fred Grant
C. Quentin Roosevelt
D. Herbert Hoover, Jr

12. Which president's son's signature appeared on Confederate dollars?

A. Smith Van Buren
B. Robert Tyler
C. Robert Lincoln
D. Dick Taylor

13. Which president was in large part responsible for the Trail of Tears, even though he had an adopted Indian son?

A. Andrew Jackson
B. William Henry Harrison
C. John Tyler
D. Zachary Taylor

14. Which president's son witnessed the signing of the Treaty of Ghent that ended the War of 1812?

A. Peter Jefferson
B. Andrew Jackson, Jr
C. John Quincy Adams
D. Payne Madison

15. Name one of the two presidential sons who were at the Appomattox Court House during the surrender of Robert E Lee?

A. Fred Grant
B. Gardi Tyler
C. Robert Lincoln
D. None of the above

Chapter 14 Answers

1. B – John Quincy Adams

2. A – Thomas Jefferson

3. B – Martin Van Buren

4. D – Margaret Wilson

* The first lady was also there to witness the signing of the Versailles Treaty. She was the *first* First Lady to attend foreign diplomatic talks.

5. C – Scott & Fanny Hayes

6. D – Webb Hayes
* The future president and first lady rescued during the Boxer Rebellion was Herbert Hoover and his wife.

7. A – Barbara & Jenna Bush

8. B – Margret Truman

9. C – The family of Gerald Ford

10. D – Eliza Monroe

11. B – Fred Grant

12. B – Robert Tyler

*Robert Tyler served as Register of the Treasury of the Confederacy and it was due to his position that his signature was on Confederate dollars.

13. A – Andrew Jackson

14. C – John Quincy Adams

15. Either B or C would be a correct answer as they were both in attendance.

B – Gardi Tyler
C – Robert Lincoln

15

Achievements of the First Family

Answers for Chapter 15 are on page 83

1. Which president's son served in the newly created Fuel Administration during WWI, for which by the end of the war he received the Distinguished Service Medal for his work?

A. Herbert Hoover, Jr
B. Harry Garfield
C. Russell Harrison
D. Robert Lincoln

2. Which president's daughter has her own jewelry and fashion line designed for young professionals?

A. Ivanka Trump
B. Doro Bush
C. Barbara Bush
D. Caroline Kennedy

3. Which president's daughter was a concert soprano?

A. Margaret Truman
B. Sasha Obama
C. Amy Carter
D. Julie Nixon

4. Which First Son was given the title "the radio genius of the industry," by an aviation trade magazine?

A. Hal Garfield
B. John Eisenhower
C. Russell Benjamin
D. Herbert Hoover, Jr

5. Which president's daughter was a successful model?

A. Patti Davis Reagan
B. Ivanka Trump
C. Tricia Nixon
D. Caroline Kennedy

6. Which First Son was an actor and worked on a soap opera and several movies with big name stars?

A. Ron Reagan
B. Don Trump, Jr
C. John Kennedy, Jr
D. Steve Ford

7. Which First daughter became U.S. ambassador to Japan after endorsing Barack Obama for president?

A. Lynda Johnson
B. Caroline Kennedy
C. Chelsea Clinton
D. Julie Eisenhower

8. Two First Sons have received the Medal of Honor. Name one of them.

A. Webb Hayes
B. Ted Roosevelt, Jr
C. John Eisenhower
D. Hal Garfield

9. Do you know which president's daughter Oprah Winfrey called 'a role model' for the 21st century woman?

A. Chelsea Clinton
B. Jenna Bush
C. Malia Obama
D. Ivanka Trump

10. Which First Daughter was Dean of Bryn Mawr?

A. Helen Taft
B. Jessie Wilson
C. Chelsea Clinton
D. Ivanka Trump

11. Which First Son while in England serving as U.S. minister of Great Britain negotiated with the King of England to keep England out of the Civil War, perhaps changing the outcome of the war?

A. Robert Lincoln
B. Dick Taylor
C. Charles Adams
D. Payne Madison

12. At the age of 25, which president's daughter became the youngest director of a publicly traded company?

A. Caroline Kennedy
B. Chelsea Clinton
C. Lynda Johnson
D. Ivanka Trump

13. Who was the 2nd First Son to follow in his father's footsteps to the Oval Office, also becoming president?

A. John Quincy Adams
B. Benjamin Harrison
C. George W Bush
D. John Kennedy, Jr

14. Which president's son worked for Herbert Hoover in the Food Administration finding a way to feed the people in Europe at the conclusion of WWI?

A. Robert Lincoln
B. Dick Taylor
C. Charles Adams
D. Robert Taft

15. Which two First Sons, already executive vice presidents of the company, were put in charge of their father's business worth billions while their father made his new office in the Oval Office?

A. Sons of Franklin D Roosevelt
B. Sons of Gerald Ford
C. Sons of George H W Bush
D. Sons of Donald Trump

Chapter 15 Answers

1. B – Harry Garfield

2. A – Ivanka Trump

3. A – Margaret Truman

4. D – Herbert Hoover, Jr

5. B – Ivanka Trump

6. D – Steve Ford

7. B – Caroline Kennedy

8. Either answer A or B would be correct.
   A – Webb Hayes
   B – Ted Roosevelt, Jr

9. D – Ivanka Trump

10. A – Helen Taft

11. C – Charles Adams

12. D – Ivanka Trump

13. C – George W Bush

14. D – Robert Taft

15. D – Sons of Donald Trump

16

Sickness & Death

Answers for Chapter 16 are on page 88

1. Which president's son was the *first* First Son to die in a foreign country?

A. Charles Adams
B. Martin Van Buren, Jr
C. Dick Taylor
D. Quentin Roosevelt

2. At the age of 12, what neurological disorder did Patsy, George Washington's stepdaughter, suffer with which eventually was the cause of her death?

A. Multiple Sclerosis
B. Stroke
C. Parkinsons Disease
D. Epilepsy

3. Who was the *first* First Daughter to die of breast cancer?

A. Nabby Adams
B. Eliza Monroe
C. Knoxie Taylor
D. Susan Ford

4. Which First Son developed a blister after a day on the tennis courts at the White House and died from blood poisioning?

A. Cal Coolidge, Jr
B. Willie Lincoln
C. Robert Taft
D. Kermit Roosevelt

5. Which First Son was diagnosed with tuberculosis and had to convalesce in a sanatorium for a year?

A. George Adams
B. Herbert Hoover, Jr
C. Lachian Tyler
D. Benjamin Pierce

6. Which president's son died in a plane crash, a plane he himself was piloting?

A. Michael Reagan
B. John Kennedy, Jr
C. Marvin Bush
D. Steve Ford

7. Two of which president's sons were with him when he was assassinated?

A. Abraham Lincoln
B. William McKinley
C. James Garfield
D. Gerald Ford

8. Which First Son shot himself committing suicide?

A. Jeff Carter
B. Franklin Roosevelt, Jr
C. Kermit Roosevelt
D. Payne Madison

9. Which president-elect's son was killed in a train accident two

months before his father's inauguration?

A. Willie Lincoln
B. Benjamin Pierce
C. Charles Adams
D. Andrew Johnson, Jr

10. Which First Son was the *first* First Family member to die in the White House?

A. Willie Lincoln
B. Peter Jefferson
C. Patrick Kennedy
D. Cal Coolidge, Jr

11. Who was the *first* president to have a First Daughter pass away while he was in office?

A. George Washington
B. John Adams
C. Thomas Jefferson
D. James Monroe

12. Which president's son was close to three presidential assassinations?

A. Robert Lincoln
B. Hal Garfield
C. Elliott Roosevelt
D. Charles Roosevelt

Chapter 16 Answers

1. B – Martin Van Buren, Jr

2. D – Epilepsy

3. A – Nabby Adams

4. A – Cal Coolidge, Jr

5. B – Herbert Hoover, Jr

6. B – John Kennedy, Jr

7. C - James Garfield

8. C – Kermit Roosevelt

9. B – Benjamin Pierce

10. A – Willie Lincoln

11. C – Thomas Jefferson

12. A – Robert Lincoln

17

After The White House

Answers for Chapter 17 are on page 92

1. Which First Daughter volunteered for the Red Cross for sixty years?

A. Ethel Roosevelt
B. Margaret Wilson
C. Patsy Washington
D. Jenna Bush

2. Which First Daughter in her old age lived in a shelter for poor women?

A. Ivanka Trump
B. Letty Tyler
C. Lynda Johnson
D. Caroline Kennedy

3. Which First Son took up oil painting after his retirement from the presidency?

A. George Washington
B. Thomas Jefferson
C. John Eisenhower
D. George W Bush

4. Which First Daughter was arrested four times for protesting?

89

A. Tiffany Trump
B. Chelsea Clinton
C. Malia Obama
D. Amy Carter

5. Which First Daughter went to live in India in an ashram and changed her name to Nishta?

A. Margaret Truman
B. Margaret Wilson
C. Amy Carter
D. Doro Bush

6. Which First Daughter or First Son lived the longest – to the age of 96?

A. Eliza Monroe
B. Caroline Kennedy
C. Alice Roosevelt
D. Lynda Johnson

7. Which First Daughter traveled giving speeches on the topic of women's right to vote?

A. Eliza Monroe
B. Pearl Tyler
C. Helen Taft
D. Barbara Bush

8. Which president's children with his second wife were all born, all seven of them, after leaving the White House?

A. Thomas Jefferson
B. Franklin D Roosevelt
C. John Tyler
D. Grover Cleveland

9. After his days of the presidency, which president and his son went to Africa to hunt big game and to collect specimens for the Smithsonian?

A. Theodore Roosevelt and son Kermit
B. Donald Trump and son Don, Jr
C. George H W Bush and son Jeb
D. Abe Lincoln and son Tad

10. Which First Daughter at the age of fifty graduated from college, finally losing the label of being the only woman in her family in the last three generations without a college degree?

A. Amy Carter
B. Jessie Wilson
C. Luci Johnson
D. Doro Bush

11. After the death of this president's illegitimate daughter it was proven by DNA that she was indeed the daughter of the president. Who was the president?

A. Bill Clinton
B. Warren Harding
C. Lyndon B Johnson
D. John F Kennedy

12. Which First Daughter was alive during the administrations of Benjamin Harrison to Jimmy Carter?

A. Ruth Cleveland
B. Mollie Garfield
C. Alice Roosevelt
D. Caroline Kennedy

Chapter 17 Answers

1. A – Ethel Roosevelt

2. B – Letty Tyler

3. D – George W Bush

4. D – Amy Carter

5. B – Margaret Wilson

6. C – Alice Roosevelt

7. C – Helen Taft

8. C – John Tyler

9. A. Theodore Roosevelt & son Kermit

10. C – Luci Johnson

11. B – Warren Harding

12. C – Alice Roosevelt

18

Books Authored By President's Children

Answers for Chapter 18 are on page 96

1. Which First Daughter wrote 'tell all' books about her family?

A. Ivanka Trump
B. Patti Davis Reagan
C. Caroline Kennedy
D. Chelsea Clinton

2. Which First Son wrote a best-selling murder mystery series?

A. Elliott Roosevelt
B. Herbert Hoover, Jr
C. Willie Lincoln
D. John Ford

3. Which First Daughter wrote several books on life in the White House, First Ladies, and White House pets?

A. Tiffany Trump
B. Jenna Bush
C. Patti Davis Reagan
D. Margaret Truman

4. Which First Son helped his father write his memoirs. The son is a military historian and wrote a book on WWII's Battle of the Bulge titled, *'The Bitter Woods: The Battle of the Bulge'*?

A. George W Bush
B. Ron Reagan
C. John Eisenhower
D. Fred Grant

5. Which First Daughter co-wrote the books '*In Our Defense: the Bill of Rights in Action*' and '*The Right To Privacy*' after learning that fewer than 59% of Americans could name the Bill of Rights?

A. Jessie Wilson
B. Caroline Kennedy
C. Julie Nixon
D. Chelsea Clinton

6. Which First Son wrote '*My Parents: A Differing View*' along with other books about his parents?

A. Cal Coolidge, Jr
B. John Eisenhower
C. Ron Reagan
D. Jimmy Roosevelt

7. The granddaughter of a president published a book based on her mother's diaries from her days in the White House. Who was the First Daughter whose diary was used for the information in the book?

A. Mollie Garfield
B. Luci Johnson
C. Martha Jefferson
D. Caroline Kennedy

8. Which First Daughter wrote the book, '*Ana's Story*' and also co-wrote two children's books with her mother the former first lady?

A. Caroline Kennedy
B. Tricia Nixon

C. Amy Carter
D. Jenna Bush

9. During the Depression in 1933, which First Daughter found herself in a financial bind, so to help her financial situation she published her autobiography?

A. Patsy Washington
B. Margaret Truman
C. Alice Roosevelt
D. Ivanka Trump

10. Which First Daughter wrote two White House mystery books whose main character was the First Daughter?

A. Susan Ford
B. Patti Davis Reagan
C. Margaret Truman
D. Barbara Bush

11. Which First Daughter wrote the book, 'Special People' about famous people she met during her time in the White House?

A. Susan Ford
B. Julie Nixon
C. Luci Johnson
D. Jenna Bush

12. Which First Daughter illustrated her father's books?

A. Amy Carter
B. Jenna Bush
C. Tricia Nixon
D. Caroline Kennedy

Chapter 18 Answers

1. B – Patti Davis Reagan

2. A – Elliott Roosevelt

3. D – Margaret Truman

4. C – John Eisenhower

5. B – Caroline Kennedy

6. D – Jimmy Roosevelt

7. A – Mollie Garfield

* The book is, 'Mollie Garfield In The White House.'

8. D – Jenna Bush

9. C – Alice Roosevelt

* The book is titled, 'Crowded Hours: Reminiscences of Alice Roosevelt Longworth.'

10. A – Susan Ford

11. B – Julie Nixon

12. A – Amy Carter

19

Who Am I?

Answers for Chapter 19 are on page 100

1. Which First Daughter was named after Tiffany's, the prestigious jewelry retailer?

A. The daughter of Donald Trump
B. The daughter of Gerald Ford
C. The daughter of John F Kennedy
D. The daughter of Richard Nixon

2. Which First Son challenged the editor of a newspaper editor to a duel for insulting his father the president?

A. George W Bush
B. Jimmy Roosevelt
C. John Tyler, Jr
D. Jacky Washington

3. Which First Daughter was nicknamed 'Princess Alice'?

A. The daughter of Theodore Roosevelt
B. The daughter of Grover Cleveland
C. The daughter of Lyndon B Johnson
D. The daughter of Benjamin Harrison

4. Which president had a son called 'Tad,' short for tadpole?

A. Ulysses S Grant
B. Abraham Lincoln

C. James Garfield
D. James Buchanan

5. Which First Daughter will hold the title, 'Most Influential First Daughter'?

A. Martha Jefferson
B. Margaret Truman
C. Chelsea Clinton
D. Ivanka Trump

6. Which First Son was part owner of the Texas Rangers baseball team?

A. Don Trump, Jr
B. Alan Coolidge
C. Jeff Carter
D. George W Bush

7. Which First Daughter ran for the Senate, but her own father refused to endorse her candidacy?

A. Amy Carter
B. Margaret Truman
C. Maureen Reagan
D. Caroline Kennedy

8. While in first grade, which First Son was teased by other children and one day punched one of the bullies. When asked where he learned to fight, he proudly answered, "The Secret Service."

A. Tad Lincoln
B. Cal Coolidge, Jr
C. John F Kennedy, Jr
D. Barron Trump

9. Which First Son was a member of the newly formed group 'Sons of the American Revolution'?

A. The son of Benjamin Harrison
B. The son of Rutherford B Hayes
C. The son of Abraham Lincoln
D. The son of Dwight D Eisenhower

10. Which First Daughter is known for being one of "the Rich Kids of Instagram"?

A. Malia Obama
B. Tiffany Trump
C. Chelsea Clinton
D. Tricia Nixon

11. Which president's son was adopted and was alive to see his father become president?

A. Jacky Washington
B. Michael Reagan
C. Andrew Jackson, Jr
D. None of the above

12. Who is the richest living First Daughter?

A. Ivanka Trump
B. Malia Trump
C. Chelsea Clinton
D. Caroline Kennedy

Chapter 19 Answers

1. A – The daughter of Donald Trump (Tiffany Trump)

2. C – John Tyler, Jr

3. A – The daughter of Theodore Roosevelt (Alice Roosevelt)

4. B – Abraham Lincoln

5. D – Ivanka Trump

6. D – George W Bush

7. C – Maureen Reagan

8. C – John F Kennedy, Jr

9. The son of Benjamin Harrison

* Members of the SAR, Sons of the American Revolution, are males whose ancestors served in the American Revolutionary War. His father's great-grandfather was a signer of the Declaration of Independence and Governor of Virginia and one of George Washington's chief adjutants.

10. B – Tiffany Trump

11. Either B or C would be correct.
    B – Michael Reagan
    C – Andrew Jackson, Jr

12. D- Caroline Kennedy

* As of the year 2017 her immediate family have a net worth of over $500 million.

20

Who Said That?

Answers for Chapter 20 are on page 104

1. Which First Daughter said: "I'll never throw away my blue jeans."

A. Malia Obama
B. Patti Davis Reagan
C. Susan Ford
D. Caroline Kennedy

2. Which First Son while hunting shot a protected species of songbird and afterward said, "Thank goodness it wasn't deer season. I might have shot a cow"?

A. Eric Trump
B. George W. Bush
C. Ron Reagan
D. Kermit Roosevelt

3. Which First Daughter said: "I hated the white House. It's like this tiny claustophic town. There are eyes and ears everywhere"?

A. Sasha Obama
B. Susan Ford
C. Chelsea Clinton
D. Patti Davis Reagan

4. Which First Daughter said: "We were well-behaved, but we

didn't deserve any Academy Awards"?

A. Tiffany Trump
B. Luci Johnson
C. Malia Obama
D. Julie Nixon

5. Which First Son said: "I was never a great intellectual"?

A. Eric Trump
B. George W Bush
C. John Eisenhower
D. Franklin Roosevelt, Jr

6. Which First Daughter said: "Determination gets you a long way"?

A. Mollie Garfield
B. Chelsea Clinton
C. Tiffany Trump
D. Lynda Johnson

7. Which First Daughter while campaigning for her father said: "Like many of my fellow millennials, I do not consider myself categorically Republican or Democrat"?

A. Ivanka Trump
B. Chelsea Clinton
C. Barbara Bush
D. Malia Obama

8. When asked what it was like to live in the White House, which First Daughter said: "I feel like it's filled with millions of ghosts. I'm not kidding. I have heard ghosts, I really have"?

A. Maureen Reagan
B. Jenna Bush
C. Amy Carter

D. Margaret Truman

9. Which First Son when approached to run for the presidency himself is said to have responded with this quote: "It seems difficult for the average American to understand that it is possible for anyone not to desire the Presidency, but I most certainly do not"?

A. John Kennedy, Jr
B. John Eisenhower
C. Robert Lincoln
D. John Quincy Adams

10. Which First Son said: "I am an unabashed atheist who is not afraid of burning in hell"?

A. Ron Reagan
B. Payne Madison
C. Chip Carter
D. George W Bush

11. Which alcoholic First Son when asked why he finally gave up drinking responded: "I'm afraid I might do something to embarrass my father"?

A. Benjamin Pierce
B. Steve Ford
C. Chip Carter
D. George W Bush

12. Which First Daughter said: "I refuse to let the opinions of others define how I see myself, how I carry myself, how I get through my days"?

A. Caroline Kennedy
B. Lynda Johnson
C. Julie Nixon
D. Ivanka Trump

Chapter 20 Answers

1. C – Susan Ford

2. B – George W Bush

3. D – Patti Davis Reagan

4. D – Julie Nixon

5. B – George W Bush

6. B – Chelsea Clinton

7. A – Ivanka Trump

8. B – Jenna Bush

9. C – Robert Lincoln

10. A – Ron Reagan

11. D – George W Bush

12. D – Ivanka Trump

If you are interested in learning more about the First Family members, or children of the presidents, read the fascinating stories of their lives in *'Children of the Presidents'* by Cheryl Pryor.

www.ingramcontent.com/pod-product-compliance
Lightning Source LLC
Chambersburg PA
CBHW060947040426
42445CB00011B/1045

* 9 7 8 1 8 8 6 5 4 1 1 6 0 *